Sportswear

Written by Alison Hawes

Contents

Football

People all over the world love football.
Millions of people play every week.
There are II players in a football team.

What to wear

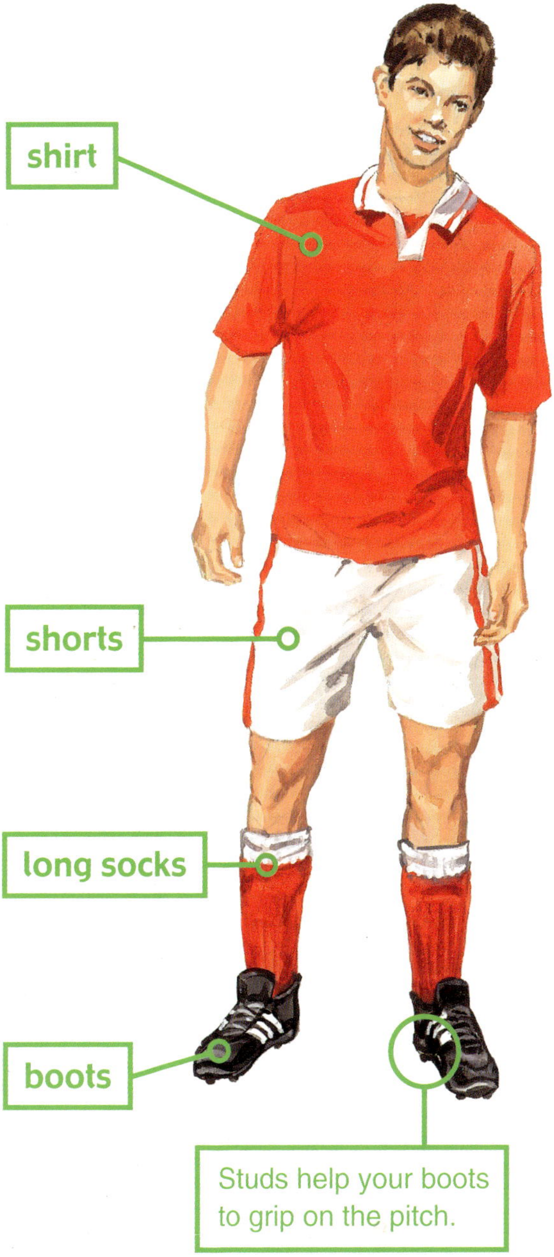

Football shirts are made of light fabric. They are cool and easy to move in.

Shin pads are worn under the socks. They protect your shins and ankles.

Skateboarding

A skate park is a good place to skateboard.
It has ramps and dips and banks for you to ride on.
Skateboarders like to do lots of tricks.

What to wear

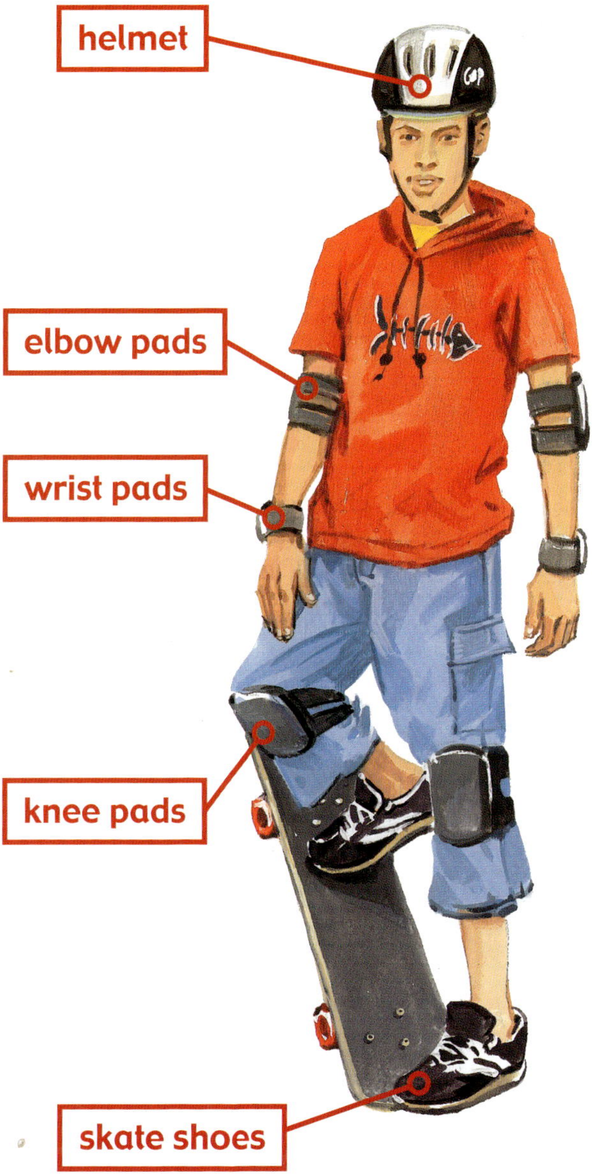

The helmet and pads protect you if you fall off!

Skateboarders wear loose baggy clothes to help them move easily.

Skate shoes are special trainers made for skateboarding.

Karate

Karate is a combat sport.

It comes from Japan.

Karate is Japanese for “open hand”.

What to wear

You cannot wear jewellery or a watch to do karate.

You have bare feet to help you grip the floor.

Karate belts come in lots of colours. If you are new to karate, you will wear a red or a white belt.

Mountain biking

A mountain bike can go over rough ground. It is made of light but strong materials.

What to wear

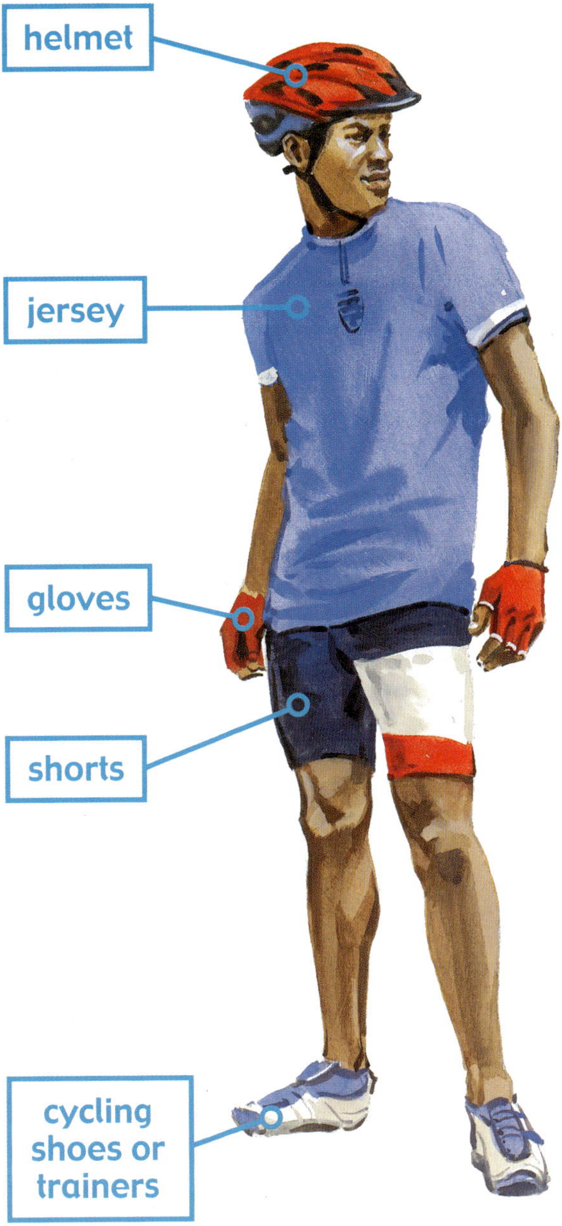

A helmet is good for all kinds of biking.

You can wear any clothes for biking but they should be light and cool.

Gloves protect your hands if you fall off!

Tennis

Tennis can be played inside or outside.
It can be played by two players or four players.

What to wear

Tennis clothes are cool and loose.
They are often white.

Holes in the shoes keep your feet cool.

Kiteboarding

Kiteboarding is a new sport. The kite pulls you over the waves. Sometimes you are lifted above the waves.

What to wear

A wetsuit keeps you warm. It does not keep you dry!

A vest is worn under the wetsuit.

Cricket

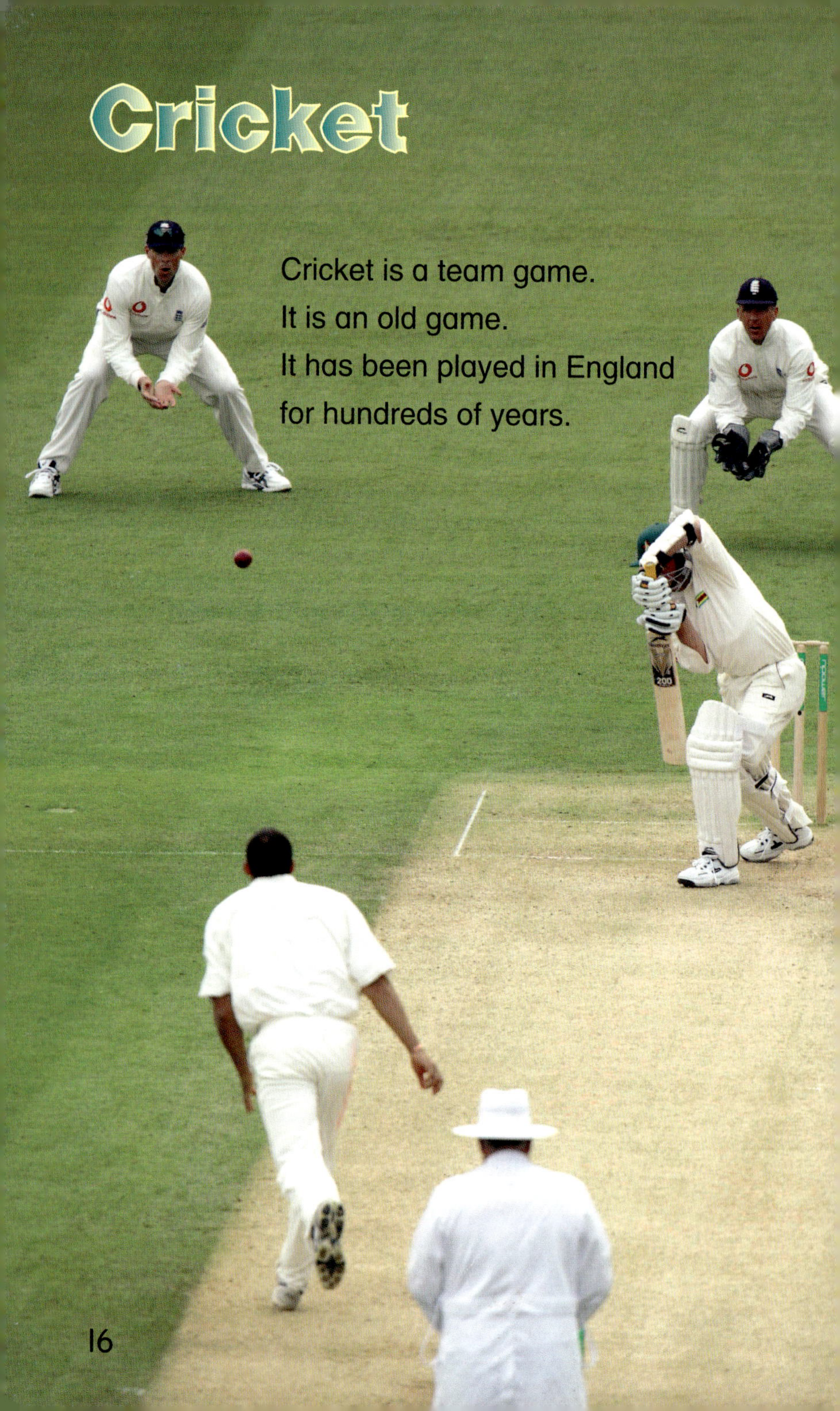

Cricket is a team game.
It is an old game.
It has been played in England
for hundreds of years.

What to wear

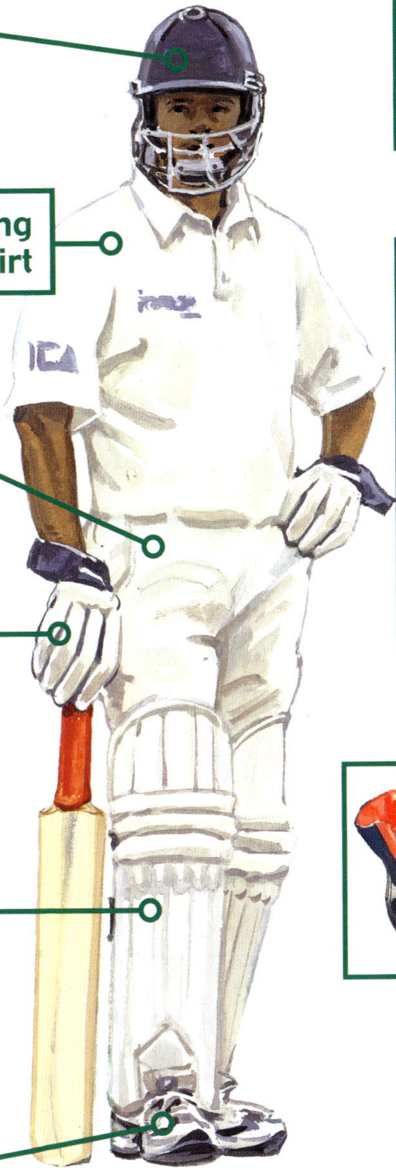

Cricket clothes are often white.

A cricket ball is very hard. The helmet, gloves and pads help protect you if the ball hits you.

Wicket keepers wear different gloves.

Caving

Cavers explore deep caves
under the ground.
Cavers go into caves in groups.
They work as a team.

What to wear

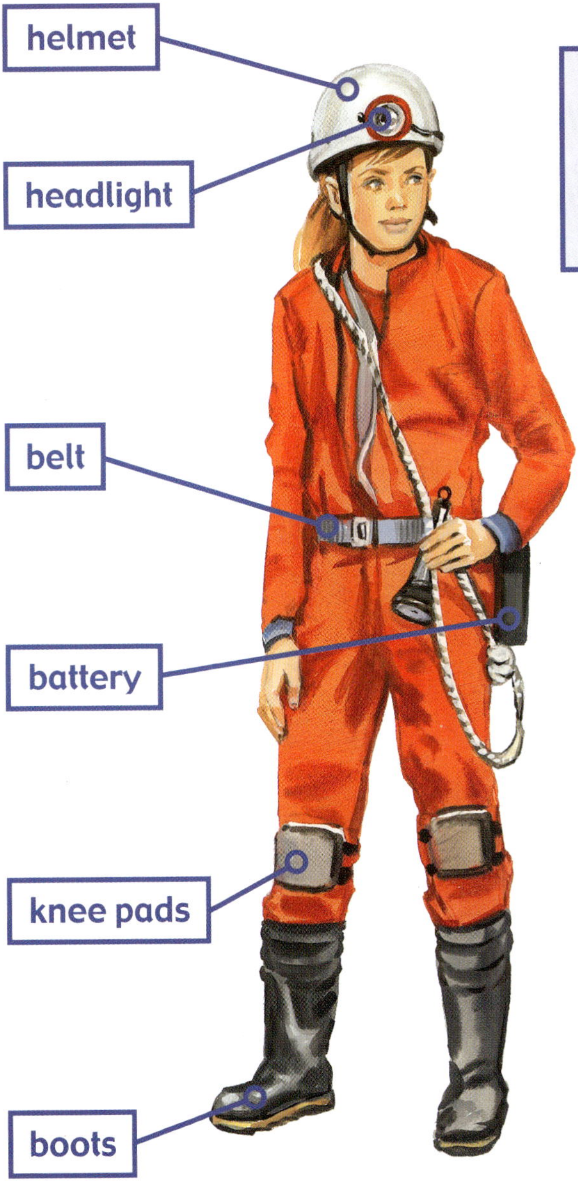

Cavers use a headlight to keep their hands free.

Some caves are cold. Cavers wear a fleece undersuit to keep them warm.

They wear a waterproof oversuit on top.

Hockey

Hockey can be played indoors and outdoors.
There are 11 players on a team.

What to wear

Some players wear a gum shield to protect their teeth.

A hockey ball can hit a goalie at up to 100 miles per hour. So a goalie wears lots of padding!

Karting

The best way to learn karting is to join a club.
If you want to race you will need to pass a test first.
You can race a kart when you are eight years old.

What to wear

A visor protects your eyes from dirt, dust and stones.

A race suit is made of strong fabric. It will not tear.

Some karters wear ear plugs. Karting can be very noisy!

Index